INTRODUCTION TO PROPERTY LAW IN INDIA

SIVA PRASAD BOSE

ISBN 979-888569561-9

Contents

Preface

Property law covers a range of conditions related to property, including its ownership, maintenance and transfer. Considering the importance and cost involved, as well as the necessity of getting a place to live, knowledge of the relevant aspects of property law is very important.

In this book, we briefly introduce various aspects of property law in India, including the Transfer of Property Act and Indian Succession Act.

It is hoped that this book will serve an an introductory guide for those who want to be aware of the applicable laws related to property in India, those who might be thinking of buying property, or those are involved in property transactions or court cases related to property.

CHAPTER ONE

What is property law

In this chapter, we discuss the concept of property laws in general terms.

1.1 Importance of property law or land law

Since the amount of land in a country like India is limited, and with limited capacity for expansion of available land for housing, the land law or property law has become more important.

Everyone needs a place to live, so property and land are basic necessities. Property prices are rising relatively more in recent years, especially in the metro cities, so for many people they are life's biggest investment in addition to being a place to stay. Many people cannot even afford to buy their own property and have to stay in rented apartments, whose rents are also increasing at a rapid pace.

Bank loans for buying land and constructing a flat is for many people the biggest loan they would take in their lives and would spend a good few years to repay. So as an investment decision, it is a major decision of one's life.

For those unfortunate enough to be involved in property disputes in the courts, these typically take up years of decades and end up costing a lot of money.

For all the above reasons and more, property law and land law are very important. It is critical to have an awareness of the prevailing property laws and how it affects one.

1.2 What does property law or land law deal with?

Property law deals with the rights and obligations one has to deal with connected with the land or property they own, rent or have a lease on, as well as the implications of transferring the same to other parties.

It deals with all aspects of the property such as mortgage loans taken from banks, taxes to be paid, registering, gifting and leasing a property, how to prove ownership of the property, how to get property as part of a will, how to pass it to one's heirs, how to rent or give property as rent, how to enable one to access basic amenities such as sunlight and water through a neighbor's land and so on.

1.3 How property can be transferred between two parties

There are multiple ways in which property transfer can happen. It can be either voluntary transfer or involuntary or compulsory transfer, and transfer when both the parties are living or when one has died and the other party gets the property by means of succession.

Depending on the type of transfer, the relevant Indian laws will apply. For example, for voluntary transfer of property between two living parties, the applicable law is Transfer of Property Act 1882, which covers sales, mortgages, leases, exchanges and gifts. For laws related to succession, the Indian Succession Act (ISA) 1925 is the applicable law. For compulsory transfers by government or due to bankruptcy and insolvency clauses, various laws can apply. Sale of Goods Act 1930 applies for sale of moveable property, which may be part of the sale of a house or apartment.

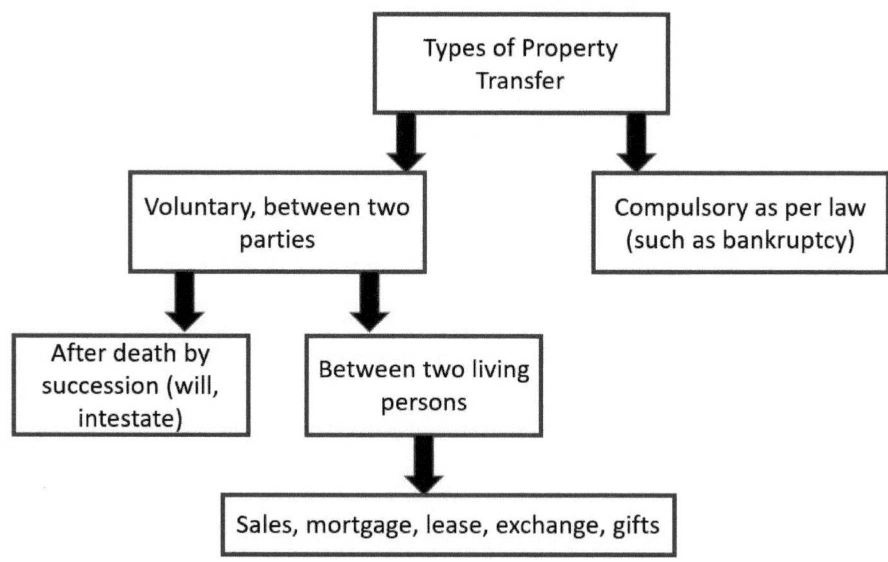

Figure 1. Types of Property Transfer

CHAPTER TWO

History of Property Law

Land law or property law has a long history. In this chapter, we study some of the main historical laws surrounding land and property in India and other countries.

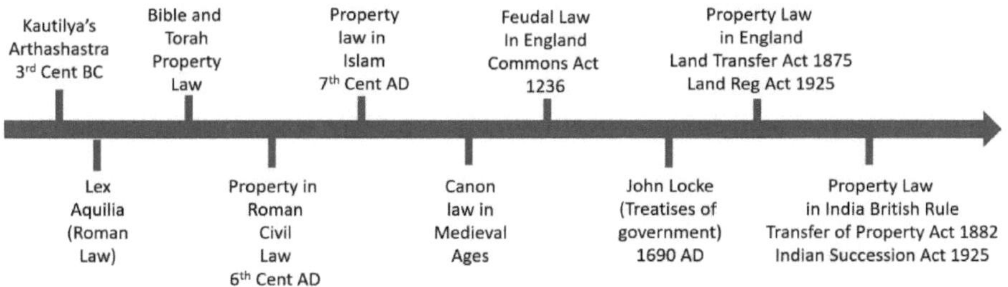

Figure 2. Evolution of Property Law

2.1 Property law in Roman times

The Romans had the concept of compensation for wrongful damage to property. They had a law called Lex Aquilia, from 3rd century BC, which provided for compensation for Roman citizens from vandalism and destruction of property. One of the provisions of that law stated "As regards things other than men and cattle which have been killed, if any one does damage to another, and unlawfully burns, breaks, or ruptures something, let him be ordered to pay its owner whatever that thing is worth in the nearest thirty days."

2.2 Property law in Kautilya's Arthashastra

Kautilya's arthashastra , also from 3rd century BC, had provisions for land management and division of inheritance. One of the property related statements in that law states "A father, distributing his property while he his alive, shall make no distinction in dividing it among his sons. Nor shall a father deprive without sufficient reason any of the sons of his share. Father being dead leaving no property, the elder sons shall show favor to the younger ones, if the latter are not of bad character."

2.3 Property law in Torah and Bible

As per the original Jewish law described in the Torah, property was only to be inherited and not sold to outsiders. Leviticus 25:23 states "But the land must not be sold beyond reclaim, for the land is Mine; you are but strangers resident with Me." Later, sale contracts were instituted.

2.4 Property as per Roman Civil Law

As per the Roman civil law instituted by Emperor Justinian in 6th Century AD, land could be owned by individuals and also transferred to others, upon following a set procedure involving witnesses and copper ignots.

2.5 Property law in Islam

Islamic law or shariah provided for inheritance of property by legal heirs. There was the concept of Waseyya or will, which stated how a person could willingly transfer one third of their property to another upon their death. The law also has the concept of Fara'id or Mirath which defined how much proportion of the deceased person's property and assets should be distributed to which heirs.

2.6 Property laws in medieval ages

In the medieval ages, canon law of the church largely governed property transactions in Europe, covering things such as wills and property acquisition. It also influenced the law on property in the post reformation era.

2.7 John Locke's views on property rights

Upon the end of feudal era, philosophers wrote about property rights. John Locke was a British philosopher who wrote about property rights in his book "The Two Treatises of Government (1690)." Locke's theory is called Labor theory of property. As per Locke, under natural law, all people have the right to "life, liberty, and estate (property)." He argued for individual property rights as natural rights.

2.8 Property law in England

English property law descended from a combination of Roman law and various feudal laws governing land and other property, including the Commons Act 1236 and Statute of Westminster 1285. After reformation, important reformed property laws were brought in England including Land

Transfer Act 1875 and Land Registration Act 1925 which provided for land registration, Wills Act 1837 that dealt with transfer of property through Wills and the Law of Property Act 1925.

2.9 Property law under British rule in India and later

With the advent of British rule in India and their creation of courts and a legal system modelled on the British legal system, property law changed in India. The Transfer of Property Act 1882 was the main act that stated the rules for transfer of moveable and immoveable property to another person. Together with the Sale of goods act 1930 (which governed sale of property) and the Indian Succession Act 1925 (governing succession of property to heirs or upon making a will), this law lays the foundation of property law in India. The same laws have survived in independent India with some modifications.

CHAPTER THREE

Transfer of Property Act 1882

In this chapter we discuss the Transfer of Property Act, which consolidates the law in India related to property transfers. The act was made in British India in 1882 and has survived in independent India with a few modifications.

THE TRANSFER OF PROPERTY ACT, 1882

ACT NO. 4 OF 1882

[17*th February*, 1882.]

An Act to amend the law relating to the Transfer of Property by act of Parties.

Preamble.—WHEREAS it is expedient to define and amend certain parts of the law relating to the transferof property by act of parties; It is hereby enacted as follows:—

CHAPTER I

PRELIMINARY

1. Short title.—This Act may becalled the Transfer of Property Act, 1882.

Commencements.—It shallcome into force on the first day of July, 1882.

Extent.—[1][Itextends[2] in the first instance to the whole of India. except [3][the territories which, immediately before the 1st November, 1956, were comprised in Part B States or in the States of], Bombay, Punjab and Delhi.]

[4][But this Act or any part thereof may by [5]notification in the Official Gazette be extended to the whole or any part of [6][the said territories] by the State Government concerned.]

[7][And any State Government may, [8]*** from time to time, by notification in the Official Gazette, exempt, either retrospectively or prospectively, any part of the territories administered by such State Government from all or any of the following provisions, namely:—

Sections 54, paragraphs 2 and 3, 59, 107 and 123.]

Figure 3. First page of the Transfer of Property Act 1882

3.1 Introduction to the Act

The Transfer of Property Act states the conditions and procedure following which a property can get transferred from one person to another. It discusses the different modes of transfer of property including sales, mortgages, leases, exchange and gifts.

In this act, property refers to both moveable as well as immoveable property. Transfer of property, according to the act, is defined as conveying a property to himself or another living person, including a company or group of individuals, in present or future. The rights, interest, ownership and/or possession of the property can be transferred.

As per the act, any person who is mentally competent and fulfills the other conditions for making a contract can transfer property to another, provided they own the property or are authorized to transfer it. They can transfer it orally or in writing, themselves or by hiring a competent lawyer.

3.2 Conditions for the transfer of property under the Act

The conditions for transfer are as follows:

- The transfer must be between two living persons
- The property being transferred should be transferable. It should not have any circumstances in which it cannot be transferred, such as chance of a heir apparent succeeding to an estate. It should not be a common asset belonging to all, such as the air or sea, that cannot be transferred.
- The person making the transfer should own the property or be competent to transfer it.
- The transfer should be done via a valid method such as sale, exchange, mortgage, lease or gift.
- The transfer cannot be in opposition to the rule of perpetuity. E.g. there should be no condition in the transfer that occurs after infinite time or the lifetime of any of the persons involved.

3.3 Interpretations under the Act

In the act, a few interpretations are stated. Immoveable property does not include standing timber, growing crops or grass. The transfer must be usually attested by two or more witnesses. Transfer of immoveable property should usually be registered under the laws of the state where the property resides. A conditional transfer, where the property is transferred upon fulfilment of a condition that is impossible, or dependent on an uncertain future event, or forbidden, or creates injury to some person, is considered to be void and the transfer is invalid.

The act also includes specific amendments for different local laws in different states of India such as Assam and Delhi.

3.4 Types of transfers under the Act

The act describes different ways in which property can be transferred. For each of these, it describes the transfer and the rights and duties of the parties to the transfer.

The different types of transfer described in the act are as follows:

- **Sale of property**: Sale means a transfer of ownership upon a price paid or promised.
- **Mortgage of immoveable property**: This refers to the transfer of interest in immoveable property as a security for a loan. The act contains detailed instructions on the rights and liabilities of a mortgager and mortgagee, how the mortgage can be redeemed, issues such as foreclosure of a mortgage, how a receiver can be appointed and so on.
- **Lease of immoveable property**: This is the transfer of the rights to enjoy a property for a specified time and upon regular payment of an amount or rent.
- **Exchange**: This is when two persons mutually transfer the ownership of one thing for another or for money only, it is called an exchange.
- **Gift**: Gift is the transfer of moveable or immoveable property by one party, called the donor, to another party called the donee, voluntarily and without any consideration, and accepted by the donee party.
- **Actionable claim**: Transfer of actionable claim means transfer of property upon a claim such as debt, from the debtor to the one they are in debt to, or who has a legally enforceable claim against them.

For each of the above types of transfers, the act lays down the procedure and defines the rights and liabilities of the parties to the transfer.

CHAPTER FOUR

Law Related to Sale of Immoveable Property

In this chapter we discuss the law related to sale of immoveable property, under the transfer of property act 1882.

4.1 Definition of sale and contract for sale

Sale is defined as transfer of ownership in exchange for a price paid. A contract for sale is a contract that defines the terms of agreement for sale between the two parties of the sale.

4.2 Rights and Liabilities of buyer and seller

The rights and liabilities are applicable for the buyer and seller, in absence of a contract to the contrary.

The seller is bound to disclose any material defect in the property, to produce documents of title to the buyer, to answer relevant questions, to execute the transfer once the price has been paid, and pay all charges and rent until the day of sale.

The seller is entitled to the rent and other interests from the property until the day of sale.

The buyer is bound to disclose to the seller any interest in the property of which they may not be aware, such as existence of oil beneath the property. He is bound to pay the purchase money to the buyer, to bear any loss to the property not caused by the seller, and pay all public charges and rent after the sale is completed.

The buyer is entitled to benefit from any increase in the value of the property post sale.

4.3 Discharge of incumbrances on sale

Incumbrances here refer to a burden on the property such as a mortgage.

In case the property has a mortgage from a third party who may apply to the court, the court may take part of the proceeds from the sale to pay off the mortgage and any further costs that may be arising and make a direct payment or transfer to the party.

CHAPTER FIVE

Law Related to Mortgage of Property

In this chapter we discuss the sections related to mortgage of immoveable property in the Transfer of Property Act.

5.1 Definition and types of mortgage

Mortgage is the transfer of interest in a property from one party (mortgagor) to another party which is a lender (mortgagee), in exchange for a loan.

For example, the buyer of the property (mortgagor) might have taken a loan from a bank (mortgagee) to pay for the sale.

Mortgage can be of different types.

- Simple mortgage means the person who takes the mortgage undertakes to pay it off by himself.
- Mortgage by conditional sale means the mortgagor sells the property on the condition that if there is a default of the payment by a certain date, then the mortgage will become absolute, but if the payment is made fully, the sale shall become void.
- Usufructuary mortgage means that the mortgagor receives rent and profits from the property until the loan has been fully paid off.
- English mortgage is where the mortgagor binds himself to pay off the mortgage and transfers the property absolutely to the mortgagee, but subject to the provision that he will re-transfer it back subject to the payment made as agreed.
- Mortgage by deposit of title deeds is where the title deeds are submitted to the creditor in return for the loan.

5.2 Rights and liabilities of the mortgagor

The mortgagor has the right to redeem the property once the loan has been repaid. They have the right to inspect the title deeds and other property documents that have been kept with the mortgagee if needed. They have the right to recover possession upon payment of the debt.

5.3 Implied contracts by the mortgagor

There is an implied contract between the mortgagor and mortgagee, which states that:

- the interest which the mortgagor professes to transfer to the mortgagee subsists, and that the mortgagor has power to transfer the same
- the mortgagor will defend, or, if the mortgagee be in possession of the mortgaged property, enable him to defend, the mortgagor's title
- the mortgagor will, so long as the mortgagee is not in possession of the mortgaged property, pay all public charges accruing due in respect of the property
- where the mortgaged property is a lease, that the rent payable under the lease, the conditions contained therein, and the contracts binding on the lessee have been paid, performed and observed down to the commencement of the mortgage

The mortgagor shall also have the power to make leases which shall be binding on the mortgagee.

5.4 Rights and liabilities of the mortgagee

The mortgagee has the right to foreclosure or sale of the property, by getting a suitable decree from the court, any time after the mortgage money debt is due to him. They have the right to sue for mortgage money in case the mortgaged property is wholly or partially destroyed or the security is rendered insufficient without any fault of the mortgagee or mortgager. They have the right to appoint a receiver for the mortgaged property. If the mortgaged property is on lease that is renewed, then the mortgagee is entitled to the new lease. They have the right to proceeds of the revenue sale in case the mortgager has failed to pay or has arrears.

Coming to liabilities of the mortgagee, if the mortgagee takes possession of the property during the mortgage, they have to manage the property, collect the rents and profits, pay taxes, conduct needed repairs, not commit any destruction on the property.

5.5 Miscellaneous items about the mortgage

The mortgagor may deposit the money that is due on the mortgage in court, after which the court may serve a notice of the deposit which, if the mortgagor agrees, will cause the discharge of the mortgage and all the documents of the mortgagor shall be returned. Once the mortgagor has returned the remaining due amount in this way, the interest on the principal money shall cease from that date.

Apart from the mortgagor, other persons with an interest in the property mortgaged, or a creditor of the mortgagor, may file a suit for redemption of the mortgage. For that, they would have the same rights as the mortgagee regarding redemption, foreclosure or sale of the property.

CHAPTER SIX

Law Related to Lease of Property

In this chapter we discuss the sections related to lease of immoveable property in the Transfer of Property Act.

6.1 Definition and types of lease

Lease of immoveable property is the transfer of the right to enjoy the property for the fixed and agreed period of time, or in perpetuity, by one party (the lessee) upon payment of a sum of money or some other thing of value to another party (lessor). The sum is called premium.

6.2 How a lease is made

A lease of immoveable property is made by a registered instrument, such as an agreement on registered paper. It can be made from year to year, or a fixed term that is more than a year, upon payment of a fixed amount or yearly rent.

6.3 Rights and liabilities of a lessor and lessee

A lessor is bound to disclose to the lessee any defects in the property before the lease is agreed. As long as the lessee follows the contract on the lease, they can hold the property for the time of the lease without interruption.

As for the lessee, of the property is destroyed by natural cause or fire or war, the lease shall become void. If the lessor does not make needed repairs to the property, the lessee may make the same and deduct its costs from the rent. The lessee is bound to pay on time the rent or premium agreed to the lessor. He is bound to restore the property to its original state on termination of the lease, barring any reasonable wear and tear. He should not insert any permanent construction on the property without the lessor's consent.

If the rent is not paid on time, the lessor can sue to eject the lessee from the property. However, if the lessee pays the arrears along with interest and costs of the lawsuit, the court may pass an order relieving the lessee from such forfeiture.

CHAPTER SEVEN

Law Related to Exchange of Property

In this chapter we discuss the sections related to exchange of immoveable property in the Transfer of Property Act.

7.1 Definition of exchange

Exchange of immoveable property is a transaction when two persons mutually transfer the ownership of one thing for another thing, or for money only.

7.2 Rights and liabilities of the parties in exchange

Both the parties have the same rights and liabilities as that of seller in a sale in respect of what they give, and buyer in a sale with what they take.

If the exchange is of money, each party has to show the genuineness of the money given.

CHAPTER EIGHT

Laws Related to Gift of Property

In this chapter we discuss the sections related to gifts of immoveable property in the Transfer of Property Act.

8.1 Introduction to gifts

Gift is the transfer of certain property without any consideration or payment. It is made by one person (donor) to another (donee) and accepted by the donee.

For a gift to be valid, the transfer has to be affected on a registered instrument signed by the donor, and attested by at least two witnesses. The gift must be of existing property, not future property.

A gift can be suspended or revoked only in certain cases, such as when if it were a contract, the contract could be rescinded.

In case of a gift, the donee cannot accept part of the gift, he has to accept the whole gift or take nothing of it.

CHAPTER NINE

Indian Succession Act 1925

In this chapter we discuss the Indian Succession Act 1925, which governs the transfer of moveable as well as immoveable property through inheritance or succession upon one's death. It was made in British Indian in 1925, but have some subsequent amendments hence.

9.1 Indian Succession Act 1925

The Indian Succession Act 1925 is an act to consolidate the law applicable to intestate (dying without a will) and testamentary succession (succession where a will is present). The purpose of this law is to present the whole body of statutory law on the subject of wills and succession in a complete form.

The ordinary meaning of the word "succession" is a transmission by law or by the will of the man to one or more persons of the property and transmission rights and obligations of a deceased person. The federal court gave its opinion on a reference in the matter of the powers of the federal legislature to provide for the levy of an estate duty in respect of property other than agricultural land, passing upon the death of any person [AIR 1944 FC 73].

THE INDIAN SUCCESSION ACT, 1925

ACT NO. 39 OF 1925[1]

[30*th September*, 1925.]

An Act to consolidate the law applicable to intestate and testamentary succession [2]***.

WHEREASit is expedient to consolidate the law applicable to intestate and testamentary succession [2]***. It is hereby enacted as follows:—

PART I

PRELIMINARY

1. Short title.—This Act may be called the Indian Succession Act, 1925.

2. Definitions.—In this Act, unless there is anything repugnant in the subject or context,—

(*a*) "administrator" means a person appointed by competent authority to administer the estate of a deceased person when there is no executor;

(*b*) "codicil" means an instrument made in relation to a Will, and explaining, altering or adding to its dispositions, and shall be deemed to form part of the Will;

[3][(*bb*) "District Judge" means the Judge of a Principal Civil Court of original jurisdiction;]

(*c*) "executor" means a person to whom the execution of the last Will of a deceased person is, by the testator's appointment, confided;

[4][(*cc*) "India" means the territory of India excluding the State of Jammu and Kashmir;]

(*d*) "Indian Christian" means a native of India who is, or in good faith claims to be, of unmixed Asiatic descent and who professes any form of the Christian religion;

Figure 4. First page of the Indian Succession Act 1925

The law of succession is the law governing the transmission of property vested in a person at his death to some other person or persons.

The act discusses the cases in which a person can die with or without making a will:

- A person dies intestate i.e. without making a will, and how their moveable and immoveable property can be divided among their various heirs starting from the closest relatives such as widow and children.
- Testamentary succession, i.e. where the deceased person has left a will before they died, specifying exactly how their property can be divided and among whom.

9.2 Summary of the act

The Indian succession act covers different grounds related to wills and other aspects of succession.

It discusses who can and cannot make a will, what is a valid will, different types of bequests, how an administrator can be appointed, how probate and letters of succession can be granted, how debts, legacies and gifts are to be paid and so on. It also covers different state amendments.

9.3 Characteristics of a will

The essential characteristics of a will are as follows:

- There must be a legal declaration of the testator's (the person making the will) intention
- The declaration must be with respect to the property of the testator
- The declaration must be to the effect that it is to operate after the death of the testator i.e. it should be revocable during the life of the testator.
- It lists the moveable and immoveable assets and states how and among whom the assets are to be divided and in what ratio
- The will must be signed and attested by two witnesses

9.4 Format of a sample will

The format of a sample will is as follows:

I, <name of testator>, son of <father's name>, aged <age in years>, resident of <address of testator>, declare this to be my last will and testament. This will cancels all my prior wills made by me.

I am in good health and possess a good mind. This will was made independently by me. No one has influenced or compelled me to make this will.

I hereby appoint <name of executor>, as the sole executor of this will.

My wife's name is <name of wife>. We have <number of children> children, whose names are as follows:

1.

2.

I have the following immovable and movable property:

1. A flat in the address _____

2. Jewelry, shares in various companies, cash and cash in bank accounts.

I declare that all the above assets are owned by me, and I have full authority over these assets.

I entrust all my movable and immovable properties to the following persons in the following ways

1. I give my bank account to my wife

2. I give my flat in the name of my son

( )

Testator's signature

Date

Signed by the testator as a last will in our presence. We have fully understood and approved the material and have signed our names as witnesses in the presence of the testator and in the presence of each other.

Name and signature of witnesses:

1.(name and signature of witness)

2. (name and signature of witness)

CHAPTER TEN

Sale of Goods Act 1930

In this chapter we go through the Sale of Goods Act of 1930, which defines the law related to the sale of goods and transfer of ownership, including moveable property but not land. It mainly focuses on contracts between the buyers and sellers.

Even though the act does not consider land, but many moveable items sold along with property could be included in this act. That is why we are discussing this act as well.

THE SALE OF GOODS ACT, 1930

ACT NO. 3 OF 1930[1]

[15*th March*, 1930.]

An Act to define and amend the law relating to the sale of goods.

WHEREAS it is expedient to define and amend the law relating to the sale of goods; It is hereby enacted as follows:—

CHAPTER I

PRELIMINARY

1. Short title, extent and commencement.—(*1*) This Act may be called the [2]*** Sale of Goods Act, 1930.

[3][(*2*) It extends to the whole of India [4][except the State of Jammu and Kashmir].]

(*3*) It shall come into force on the 1st day of July, 1930.

2. Definitions.—In this Act, unless there is anything repugnant in the subject or context,—

(*1*) "buyer" means a person who buys or agrees to buy goods;

(*2*) "delivery" means voluntary transfer of possession from one person to another;

(*3*) goods are said to be in a "deliverable state" when they are in such state that the buyer would under the contract be bound to take delivery of them;

(*4*) "document of title to goods" includes a bill of lading, dockwarrant, warehouse keeper's certificate, wharfingers' certificate, railway receipt, [5][multimodal transport document,] warrant or order for the delivery of goods and any other document used in the ordinary course of business as proof of the possession or control of goods, or authorising or purporting to authorise, either by endorsement or by delivery, the possessor of the document to transfer or receive goods thereby

Figure 5. First page of the Sale of Goods Act 1930

10.1 Summary of the Act

The Sale of Goods Act 1930 defines a contract for a sale of goods between a buyer and a seller, where the ownership of an item is transferred from the seller to the buyer upon payment of a price. The term goods refers to "every kind of movable property other than actionable claims and money; and includes stock and shares, growing crops, grass, and things attached to or forming part of the land which are agreed to be severed before sale or under the contract of sale."

Along with the ownership and rights, any risks and liabilities associated with the item are also transferred from the seller to the buyer. the act covers existing goods as well as goods to be transferred in the future.

The act defines what is a contract of sale and the various conditions associated with the contract. It also covers various cases where the goods are faulty or the contract conditions are not met. It covers the rights of the buyers and the sellers, as well as special conditions like damaged goods and auctions.

CHAPTER ELEVEN

Law on Easements

In this chapter, we discuss what are easements and what is the the Indian law on easements.

11.1 What is easement

Easements refer to partial rights of a neighbor on another's property, other than ownership. It is the right to temporarily enter and use the neighbor's property without possessing it. They are usually linked to the enjoyment of a different neighboring property, as in the rights of easement will enable the owner of the other property to fully enjoy the property.

Examples of easements include rights of way, or right to transfer essential resources such as water or fuel, through another's private property.

Easements are of two types:

- Positive easement refers to allowing to use another's property. Examples include giving another the rights of way through one's property.
- Negative easement refers to restrictions or restraints upon the owner of the property to certain aspects of using the property, so that the other party does not face difficulty. Examples include right to access water or sunlight.

11.2 What is the Indian law on easements

The Indian Easements Act 1882 consolidates the Indian law on easements.

THE INDIAN EASEMENTS ACT, 1882

ACT NO. 5 OF 1882[1]

[17*th February*, 1882.]

An Act to define and amend the law relating to Easements and Licenses.

Preamble.—WHEREAS it is expedient to define and amend the law relating to Easements and Licenses; It is hereby enacted as follows:—

PRELIMINARY

1. Short title.—This Act may be called the Indian Easements Act, 1882.

Local extent.—It extends[2] to the territories respectively administered by the Governor of Madras in Council and the Chief Commissioners of the Central Provinces and Coorg;

Commencement.—and it shall come into force on the first day of July, 1882.

2. Savings.—Nothing herein contained shall be deemed to affect any law not hereby expressly repealed; or to derogate from—

(*a*) any right of the [3][Government] to regulate the collection, retention and distribution of the water of rivers and streams flowing in natural channels, and of natural lakes and ponds, or of the water flowing, collected, retained or distributed in or by any channel or other work constructed at the public expense for irrigation;

(*b*) any customary or other right (not being a license) in or over immovable property which the Government, the public or any person may possess irrespective of other immovable property; or

(*c*) any right acquired, or arising out of a relation created, before this Act comes into force.

[4][**3. Construction of certain references to Act 15 of 1877 and Act 9 of 1871.**—All references in any Act or Regulation to sections 26 and 27 of the Indian Limitation Act, 1877[5] or to sections 27 and 28 of Act No. 9 of 1871[6] shall, in the territories to which this Act extends, be read as made to sections 15 and 16 of this Act.]

Figure 6. First page of the Indian Easements Act 1882

The act defines what is an easement, how they are acquired and by whom they can be imposed, how the easement rights can become extinct or revoked and how they can be revived. They also cover temporary licenses given by one party to another, allowing them to perform certain actions related to using a property.

CHAPTER TWELVE

Conclusion

In this book, we have introduced and discussed the various aspects of property law or land law in India and how property can be transferred from one person to another.

We covered the history of how property law evolved in India and other countries. We then discussed relevant laws related to property in India, focusing on the Transfer of Property Act 1882. We also covered other relevant acts for property including Indian Succession Act 1925, Indian Easements Act 1882 and Sale of Goods Act 1930. We have briefly covered rights and liabilities of the parties under these acts.

Since property is simultaneously a basic necessity and one of life's biggest investments for a common man, as well a major source of headache if one is fighting long pending property cases in the courts, it is useful for all of us to be familiar with the laws and procedures related to it.

About The Authors

Siva Prasad Bose is an author of various introductory guidebooks related to aspects of Indian laws. He is currently retired after many years of service in Uttar Pradesh Power Corporation Limited. He received his engineering degree from Jadavpur University, Kolkata and has a law degree from Meerut University, Meerut. His interests lie in the fields of family law, civil law, law of contracts, and any areas of law related to power electricity related issues.

Joy Bose is a software engineer and a data scientist by profession.

Other Books By Siva Prasad Bose

Introduction to Wills and Probate

Senior Citizens Abuse in India

Introduction to negotiable instruments

Introduction to marriage laws in India

Neighbor Problems in India and what to do about them

Managing Court Cases with Mental Strength

Delays in Court Cases in India

Introduction to Patents and Patent Law in India

Printed by Libri Plureos GmbH in Hamburg,
Germany